The Truth About You

Who You Are and Why You're Here on Earth

Also by Brad "Little Frog" Hudson

Shamanic Depossession and Other True Healing Miracles

Vision Quests: True Stories From the Wilderness

WHO YOU ARE AND WHY YOU'RE HERE ON EARTH

BRAD "LITTLE FROG" HUDSON

Little Frog Publishing
Westford, Massachusetts
2014

First Printing: 2014

ISBN 978-0-9908368-2-7

Little Frog Publishing
35 Carlisle Road
Westford, MA 01886

www.LittleFrogHealing.com

Ordering Information:

Special discounts are available on quantity purchases by corporations, associations, educators, and others. For details, contact the publisher at the above listed address.

U.S. trade bookstores and wholesalers: Please contact Little Frog Publishing at 978-590-0186 or email LittleFrogHealing@gmail.com.

To my wife, Karen, for her love and support.

Contents

FOREWARD

As Mother Earth and her inhabitants continue to move toward the fifth dimensional ascension, more and more people are searching for answers to their most pressing questions. Who am I? Where did I come from? Why am I here? What happens when I die?

These are important questions. The answers may be life changing for many people.

While there are a zillion books available today regarding every aspect of metaphysics, until now there wasn't a single book that answered ALL the questions.

This is my attempt to do just that.

My goal was to create a short, easy-to-read, handy reference book. Within I have addressed every concern that an old soul could have concerning life, death and the afterlife. After all, if you are not an old soul, most likely you would not be reading this. Young and middle aged souls are generally not interested in these questions.

Some of the information herein is repeated in several different chapters. This is because everything is interrelated, and some information is so important it needs to be repeated many times.

I am a shamanic practitioner and a multidimensional energy healer. I died briefly in 1983. Much of the information within comes from my personal experiences in ordinary and non-ordinary reality. The rest comes from the extensive reading I did on the topics at hand- over 400 books- and the hundreds of individuals I spoke with to satisfy my own questions, the same questions I address in this book.

This is the information as I understand it. My answers are brief. An in-depth explanation of each topic would require at least one book per topic. It is my hope that this small book will create conversations between you and your friends, meaningful conversations that will motivate you to learn more about these subjects. If you want to pursue additional information regarding a chapter topic, I include references with brief descriptions at the end of the book. I highly encourage you to read every reference listed.

Blessings of Spirit,

Brad "Little Frog" Hudson
Westford, MA
September 2014

CHAPTER ONE- THE TRUTH ABOUT YOU

You are a ball of energy consciousness, temporarily masquerading as matter in a three dimensional world of illusions.

You have incarnated hundreds, if not thousands, of times on this Earth. Each time you volunteered to be here. Prior to every incarnation, including this one, you chose the life you wanted to experience, along with the lessons to be learned. You incarnate, along with other members of your "soul group", according to a well defined plan worked out prior to your incarnation.

You have a group of fellow energy beings, known as your "Guides", around you and ready to assist you at all times while on Earth.

"Death" is merely a transition from this dimension to your home dimension upon the shutdown of your human body at a predetermined time.

That's pretty much it, in a nutshell.

Whoa, slow down you say. None of this makes any sense! "I've never heard any of this before in my life!" you protest.

That's right, you've never heard about this because we are all born with the "veil of amnesia". The veil permits each of us to come into this world with no prior knowledge of our true identities or our connection with Source (also commonly known as Spirit, the Creator, or All That Is).

The Earth is a grand experiment in our Universe. Earth is the only planet where the inhabitants, humans in this case, are born with the veil of amnesia. The veil accelerates the learning process necessary for our souls' evolution back to Source. All other inhabitants in our Universe understand their connection with Source and thus do not share the Earthly duality which causes our negative emotions.

However, as idyllic as that may sound for our extraterrestrial friends, the lack of duality elsewhere inhibits and greatly slows their learning curve. How does one explain the concept of anger to someone who has never experienced it? What you learn in just a few lifetimes on Earth may take thousands of years to learn on a different planet.

In addition to the veil of amnesia, you are also born with "free will". Even though your life is meticulously planned prior to your birth, you still have the ability to make decisions that change the course of your planned life. Each time you exercise your free will, you create another parallel timeline where you live out the option you declined to take. Free will does not affect the other residents of our Universe, because they are fully aware of their connection to Source, and consequently make all their decisions based upon what will best strengthen that connection.

Confused? I thought so. It's easier if we start at the beginning...

CHAPTER TWO- IN THE BEGINNING

Before anything existed in any universe or dimension, there was Source, also known as Spirit, All That Is, the Great Mystery, or the Creator (I dislike using the terms "God", or "Allah", as they are too politically charged). Source is an incredibly vast consciousness, comprised only of Love, far beyond anything our minds can comprehend.

One day, possibly while playing cosmic solitaire, Source devised a plan to learn more about Itself. Source decided to create replicas of Itself, an infinite number of them. "Souls", It called them. Each one will be a perfect replica of Its consciousness, albeit on a much smaller scale.

But what will these souls do? Source made another decision. It will create matter from Love energy, and from this matter It will create a place called a "Universe". This Universe will have an infinite number of locations for the souls to exist and interact with each other. Source will then learn from observing all the interactions of Its souls.

Source thought the Big Bang into existence, and observed the formation of an infinite number of galaxies, star systems and planets. Life, in an infinite number of forms, began on an infinite number of planets. Now Its souls had a wide choice of places to live, visit and interact with one another.

One problem though. While the souls can interact with each other easily enough, as energy beings it would be problematic for them to interact with their physical environments. So Source devised a method whereby souls can place their consciousnesses inside creatures native to their chosen planet in order to experience existence as a physical being rather than an energy being. Now all that remains is to grow, learn and interact with your fellow physical beings.

It's all coming together now...

CHAPTER THREE- UNIVERSAL LAWS

Love is the only thing that exists anywhere. Love is the energy of the Universe. It comes directly from Source. Without Love there is nothing. Source used Love to create you and the Universe around you.

Matter comes from energy, and energy is Love, so therefore matter is Love too.

Energy is alive, it is sentient. Energy has a vibration. Everything is made from energy, so everything is alive and has a vibration- a unique vibration. You have a unique vibration. It's your fingerprint. It identifies you.

And since energy is sentient, everything has a consciousness. Animals, vegetation, rocks, houses, cars, EVERYTHING has a consciousness. Every cell in your body has a consciousness.

You create your own reality through your thoughts and interactions with everything in your environment. Your thoughts are reflected back to you by your environment. Your thoughts ARE your environment.

If you love your car, your car will return that love to you and you will experience very few, if any, breakdowns. However, if you dislike your car, your car will pick up on that and respond in a negative manner, and you will experience many problems with your car.

I recently purchased a vintage Martin acoustic guitar that had been split in half. The damage had been professionally repaired, but no one wanted the guitar because of the damage. It sounded incredible, but the seller warned me that it needed new tuning machines, an expensive replacement, because it always went out of tune while playing. I fell in love with it, bought it, and took it home. At first it was constantly out of tune, but as I played it and showered it with Love every day, it began to stay in tune. Now I rarely have to tune the guitar- it stays in perfect tune by itself, and I never touched the tuning machines on the headstock. This is the power of thoughts and Love!

Thoughts are things; they are energy. Every thought has a unique vibration, just like every person has a unique vibration. It's how the Universe tells everything apart. Every thought you think, whether positive or negative, flows out into the Universe as a vibration. The primary job of the Universe is to match the vibrations of your thoughts with the appropriate vibrations needed for manifestation. This is called the "Law of Attraction". The Universe matches positive thought vibrations with similar positive manifesting vibrations. Unfortunately, the Universe does the same for negative thoughts, and manifests them into negative events too.

For example, if you see a house you really love, but after looking at the price tag you say "I will never be able to afford that house", the Universe will do its job and make sure you can never afford to purchase that house. After all, that is the vibration you put out into the Universe- "I can't afford it"- so the Universe matches that negative vibration with the appropriate negative result.

The Universe will match positive vibrations with positive results. If, after seeing the same house, you say "I love that house and I will own that house ", the Universe will put into motion the manifestation of that result. Don't worry about "how" it will happen. The "how" questions belong to the Universe. You may know only a few ways to manifest ownership of that house, but the Universe has an infinite number of ways to make this come true. So, by putting your intention of buying that house out into the Universe, you have started the process of manifestation. The Universe is now once again doing its assigned job of figuring out how to make this thought vibration a reality for you.

You can assist the Universe by taking appropriate steps towards the realization of your goal. You have already stated your intention, so follow that by taking action. Start with baby steps. Forget about the "hows". You never have to figure out "how" to do something. It is enough that you want to do it. Let the Universe do its thing.

Continuing with the real estate example, envision yourself living in that home. Picture yourself sleeping in the bedroom, eating in the kitchen, relaxing in the living room. Do this every day, multiple times if possible. If the house is on the market, find a realtor, tour the home, talk to mortgage companies, go through all the steps as if you are actually purchasing this house. If the house is not on the market, create a vision board to help you manifest the outcome you desire. Ask a realtor to let you know if the house comes on the market. Write the owners a letter telling them how much you love their home and you would like to purchase it if they ever want to sell it. These steps help the Universe calculate how you can acquire that house. And one day all the pieces of the puzzle will fall into place, and you will have your new house.

"Karma" is another law of our Universe. Karma is the result of an individual's actions in determining the future of that individual.

Karma can be both good and bad. For instance, volunteer work in a soup kitchen serving homeless people results in good, or positive karma, which may play out in that life or a future lifetime. Treating one's employees like slaves results in bad karma, ensuring that individual some kind of payback down the line. The results of karma do not have to play out in the same lifetime as incurred. It is different for each soul.

In order for karma to work properly, there must be duality and time. The Earth is a world of duality, or opposites-hot/cold, bad/good, night/day. Karma ensures that the duality of right/wrong is balanced out over the course of your lifetimes on Earth.

Without the concept of time, karma cannot exist. Time must lapse between the original event and the payback. A causation must occur, effecting a rectification of events after a period of time. After many, many lifetimes, each soul understands that certain actions lead to negative consequences, and those actions are subsequently avoided going forward. Karma is balanced.

Free will is the third dominant law of the Universe. Free will is the ability to make any choice you want, regardless of whether it is right or wrong.

Prior to incarnating each time, you know exactly how your life will proceed, what lessons you will learn, and who will be the major players in your life. However, thanks to the veil of amnesia, once you are born you no longer remember the details of your life-to-be, so you are free to make choices that conflict with the original plan. Older souls learn to listen to their inner voice, or intuition, and therefore avoid the problems associated with free will. If you exercise too much free will, you may find yourself returning in your next life to learn the same lessons you should have learned in this life.

But that is OK. You have eternity to get it right.

CHAPTER FOUR- WHO ARE YOU?

You are energy with a consciousness. You have been around for eons, and have lived anywhere from hundreds to thousands of lives on Earth. Most likely, because you are reading this book, you are an old soul. Old souls are very interested in why they are here, and their purpose for being here. Middle aged souls are materialistic; they are more concerned with keeping up with the neighbors than with their life's path. Young souls are all about me, me, me.

You were given consciousness by Source when It created you from pure Love. All energy was created by Source from Love. Therefore, you are conscious Love.

You never lose your personality. It is what makes you uniquely you. You spend eons adjusting and perfecting it by applying the lessons learned in each lifetime. You may enter different lifetimes with different mindsets depending on what you have set out to learn, but your core personality is always yours.

When not incarnated, you live in another dimension with your soul group of 20-30 other souls. You have been with them forever, and you are all best friends. Your group incarnates together, with each soul taking a different role during each lifetime. Your son in this lifetime may be your mother in the next lifetime. Souls who choose not to incarnate with the group act as guides for those incarnated.

Each time you transition from Earth to home, you go to the Hall of Records, also known as the Akashic Records, where a complete record is kept of every incarnation you have experienced. You undergo a Life Review, where your most recent life is played back to you in its entirety, like a movie. During this Review you experience not only your own emotions but also the emotions of the people you interacted with during your life. This provides a unique way of understanding and learning the impact you made on your fellow humans throughout each lifetime.

At some point you begin to contemplate voluntarily returning to Earth for another go at life. You are offered a choice of parents, and shown how you will look and what your life will be like under each scenario. Once you make a decision regarding your parents, the other members of your soul group make their decisions regarding what roles they will assume in your life. Everyone decides what lessons each will learn. In many cases, a soul will volunteer to depart Earth at an early age, through one of many means- a car accident, fatal disease, murder- so its fellow souls can experience the powerful emotions associated with that action. Life on Earth can be very difficult at times, and you are here to experience everything.

Because of the veil of amnesia, you are given keys to the crucial points and events in your life to help you make the decisions that are the most beneficial to your learning. Theses triggers help you identify people like your spouse, your best friend, and what jobs you take. Listening to your inner voice helps. That voice comes from your higher self, which is in broad terms the portion of your consciousness that remains behind when you incarnate. It is very advanced, and it helps guide you through your life on Earth. As you get better at listening to it, you notice life gets easier.

You are given specific lessons to learn during each incarnation. It is usually one or two things to learn, but they take an entire lifetime, or more, to absorb. Because of the nature of duality on Earth, most of the lessons revolve around negative emotions and how to overcome them with Love.

When you are in your home dimension, it is impossible to learn about negatives like anger, guilt and hate, because nothing but love and joy exist there. Reading about these emotions doesn't accurately convey the feelings aroused by them. It is like trying to explain to someone what it is like to have a child if he or she is childless. It is impossible to convey how a child changes your life without the actual experience.

In order to better understand Love, you must better understand the negative emotions. And as you work your way through the negative emotions, you learn more about forgiveness and Love. Hence, you incarnate on Earth to fully understand and appreciate emotions like hate, anger, guilt and shame. You return home with a renewed understanding of Love.

At the end of the day, you are one with every other person here on earth. Source created all souls from Its Love. Each soul is a part of Source. We are all part of one huge collective consciousness, but at our present level we identify ourselves as individual souls. We don't realize that in our physical incarnation, we are all the same. We are all part of the same consciousness.

You and everyone on the Earth are one and the same. You interact with yourself in the form of others over and over every day. Your thoughts form your reality, and your reality is reflected back to you in the form of others. You continue these interactions until you eventually reach a state of Love for everyone. That means forgiving everyone around you and understanding that everyone and everything is a reflection of you. It is especially important to forgive and Love yourself too. When this is accomplished, you have learned the true meaning of Love.

CHAPTER FIVE-
WHY YOU ARE HERE ON EARTH

The Earth is a unique experiment in our universe. Only on Earth are you born with the veil of amnesia, which means you don't remember your connection to Source once you've incarnated. Your mind was wiped clean when you were born. As a result, you have to deal with negative emotions, which only exist because you no longer recall you are a perfect being, a smaller version of Source itself.

It takes a brave soul to incarnate on Earth. The other civilizations in our universe call Earth the "insane asylum of the universe." You are the equivalent of the elite Special Forces in the military, because of the difficulty of this mission and the fact that you volunteered to be here. Only a tiny percentage of all souls ever volunteer to incarnate on Earth. Because Earth is most difficult, you learn your lessons the fastest while here.

Lessons? What lessons? Wasn't I created as a perfect being? Yes, you were, but in order to fully comprehend the meaning of Love, you must explore all facets of Love- the good and the bad. Earth provides a wonderful setting to learn about duality, the relationship of opposites. Good/bad, hot/cold, and love/hate are just a few examples of duality. To fully explore the countless types of interactions with other humans, and learn how everything relates to Love, requires thousands of incarnations on Earth. Every lifetime draws you one step closer to reuniting with Source, which is your ultimate goal.

You are here to experience a life of joy and love, to help your fellow man, and to do whatever it is that makes your heart sing. Somehow we have moved away from this goal as a society. In today's world, we are all so busy just trying to live that we have lost touch with what is really important. The daily struggle of putting food on your family's table and a roof over their heads has taken priority over the discovery of what makes you most happy in your world.

Some people discover what makes their heart sing at an early age, and they go through life doing what they love. This brings them joy every day, and this joy manifests into abundance for them, because they are not focused on how things will happen. They allow things to happen in their lives.

Most of us have a job to make money, and then we have a hobby we love. We see the job as a necessary evil because we need money to survive. Our hobbies bring us joy, but that is limited joy because we don't believe it will ever make us enough money to pay our bills each month. We are too focused on the "hows" of the situation- How will we locate our customers, How will we grow our business?

I had a friend who worked at a lumber yard. His passion was restoring old furniture. He would drive around on trash day and pick up furniture people were throwing away, take it home and work on it at nights and on weekends. This brought him great pleasure. He did it because he loved it. He began putting pieces he restored in his home, and his friends noticed his work, and asked him if he could work on some of their furniture. Before he knew it, my friend quit his job at the lumber company and was restoring furniture full time, making a very good living. This is a terrific example of how the Love and joy put into a hobby results in the hobby becoming the primary source of income. It no longer feels like work, because you Love doing it. The vibrations you put out into the Universe caused the Universe to bring you everything you needed to turn your hobby into a business that doesn't feel like work. You now have Love, joy and abundance in your life. This is how it works.

Along the way you will learn a few lessons during each lifetime. As you will see, the Universe is wired to help you achieve everything you want through the manifestation of your thoughts.

CHAPTER SIX- YOUR PATH THROUGH LIFE

The journey you take through each lifetime, from birth to death, is called your path, or your spiritual path. You can never get it wrong. It is always perfect.

It is perfect because it comprises every possible probability in each lifetime. Because of free will, your future is not set in stone. The basic parameters of your life are decided upon before you are born, but you have the ability to make decisions that veer from the stated objectives of each lifetime. This is what makes physical life interesting!

Each time you make a decision, you create a new Universe for the road not taken, and a parallel you lives out that life. And that parallel you makes decisions too, creating even more Universes. So by the time you die, you have created millions of parallel Universes that play out every possible scenario for that lifetime. You learn from all of them.

Your path is your unique journey through every lifetime. It is a never-ending quest for knowledge, for this knowledge feeds your lessons and enables your soul to grow.

The goal of your path is to bring you joy and love through your experiences and interactions with others. It is not selfish to make decisions based upon this; in fact, it is desired to make your decisions based upon the amount of joy and love you will experience.

Your path will continually intersect with other people's paths throughout each lifetime. Some of these crossings will be once and done. Some are karmic in nature, and will cease when the karmic lessons are completed. Some will intersect repeatedly, and these people become important in your life. As a result of these interactions, certain people become your spouse, your best friend, even your enemy. While it is easy to imagine the lessons learned from loved ones, the lessons learned from your enemies are more difficult to absorb. Enemies teach you great lessons about love and forgiveness once you realize why they are in your life. Thank them for their lessons just like you thank your loved ones, and they too become loved ones.

You are not responsible for anyone's path but your own. Just as you are responsible for your own Love and joy, everyone else is responsible for their own Love and joy. This is not being selfish; rather, it is following your path through each physical incarnation. This is one of the most difficult lessons to learn. When you see your children making "wrong" decisions, you want to jump in and help them. But all you can do is provide them with the tools they need to get through life. You cannot live their lives for them. They must walk their own path through each lifetime, the same as you.

When you walk your path with the intent of Love and joy, the Universe provides you with wonderful experiences. Things happen that you never could have imagined, because you are now letting the Universe take care of the "hows". You meet fantastic people, have terrific experiences, and you are always moving forward. We all know people like this. You can be one of them too.

CHAPTER SEVEN- GUIDES

You are never alone on Earth.

You have a team of souls, called guides, who are with you always. Some of these guides come from your soul group. Others are assigned to you for specific periods of time, to help with specific lessons. You also have a group of angels watching over you for each lifetime on Earth. There is a third group of souls who come in and out of your life just to observe you in action. These souls are your fans, who learn by watching you. Some have never experienced physical incarnation on Earth, and therefore they learn valuable lessons from observing you during each lifetime.

When you feel alone and are having a difficult time with something, know that you have many, many beings around you to provide support. In fact, during your darkest times, when you think you are the most alone, that is the time you have the most beings are around you, helping and observing. They can see you, but you cannot see them. They can hear you. You can hear them by realizing the ideas that just pop into your head, or things that you instinctively know, come from them as well as your higher self.

Your support beings always hear your requests for assistance.

While your guides and angels are here to assist you, they can only do so when you ask. So it is critically important to ask them for help when you need it. The two biggest misconceptions about your guides and angels are 1) you are bothering them by asking; and 2) it must be an emergency to ask.

You are not bothering them by asking, nor does it have to be an emergency to ask them. They are with you because they WANT to help you. They know how difficult it is on Earth. Many of them have already completed their tours of duty on Earth. They are waiting to support you. Ask them a hundred times each day, no problem.

Ask them for help with anything, from finding a good parking spot at the hottest restaurant to helping you with a job interview. Say you are a chef, and having trouble with a particular recipe. Ask your guides and angels for help. Most likely they will bring in a soul who was a terrific chef at one time on Earth to help you. Suddenly you feel inspired to try certain spices or a different cooking technique, and, voila, your problem is solved. That inspiration was a little nudge from the specialist brought in for that particular problem. We've all had experiences where we suddenly just know something we didn't know before, and that information comes from our support team. The more aware you are of your support, the more help you can call upon, and the less problems you will encounter. Life on Earth is difficult enough as it is, don't make it more difficult by ignoring your help!

There will be times when you don't receive help. When this occurs, it means that you are dealing with an important lesson that you need to figure out on your own. You have not been abandoned by your support team! Your team knows when they can provide assistance and when they must step back. After all, you and they worked out all of this prior to your physical incarnation. The veil of amnesia has ensured you cannot remember this.

Otherwise, your guides and angels are basically sitting around playing cards, bored, waiting for you to request assistance. Give them something to do! Put them to work, they want you to ask for help!

Tom T. Moore, in his book, "The Gentle Way," identifies a specific way to ask for help from your angels that was given to him years ago by one of his angels. You say out loud, "I want to request a most benevolent outcome for (fill in the blank) please, thank you." Be sure to give the angels enough lead time to make the proper arrangements. You can use this hundreds of times each day, for anything. Put your angels to work!

CHAPTER EIGHT- E=MC²=LOVE

Before there was anything, there was only Love. Source used Love to create everything during that split second called the Big Bang. Where there was once emptiness, there was now energy transmuted into matter.

All energy carries with it a vibration. You have a unique vibration that identifies you as you. Your vibration is exactly like a fingerprint. For instance, long distance healers locate your spirit body through your vibrations.

Every thought you think has a vibration, and the universe matches the vibrations of your thoughts with the appropriate vibrations of occurrences. This is how you create your reality. If you think negative thoughts, you will experience a difficult reality. If you think positive thoughts, you will experience a much more pleasant reality.

So your reality is actually a perfect reflection of yourself. This is a very important concept. You create your reality through your thoughts. You project your thoughts into the Universe. The Universe responds with the appropriate matching reality through the vibrations of your thoughts. If you are in a good mood, your day is pleasant and fun. If you are in a bad mood, everything goes wrong.

Love is the root of everything. One of your major lessons is to discover this at some point along your path. By changing negative emotions into loving emotions, you improve your life immensely. Realize that everything you see around you is a direct reflection of your thoughts. Have you ever been in a hurry to get somewhere, and you hit every red light along the way? Yet when you are not in a hurry, you get there faster? That is the Universe telling you to change your thoughts, to approach each situation with love.

How does this happen? The next time someone upsets you, stop for a second. Instead of getting angry at that person, realize that everything is a learning experience, and reverse the situation by treating that person with love. When you apply this you will see how quickly that person changes his or her attitude. Suddenly the situation is changed for the better, the anger is gone, and your blood pressure is still normal. Send the person love and forgiveness, then send yourself love and forgiveness. Thank the person for the lesson you learned.

Practice this every day and you will soon see a major difference in your life. Conflicts disappear. You will find that people are nicer to you everywhere you go. You are smiling all the time. You are in the flow.

Slowly the negative emotions slip away, leaving only a constant feeling of joy and love. You look forward to each new day and the joy that it brings. Then prepare yourself, for this is when the magic kicks in through the manifestation of your thoughts into things that make you happy.

CHAPTER NINE-MANIFESTATION

You are perfect. You were born perfect, spawned from Source's love. Source is perfect, therefore you are perfect too. As such, you too are a creator.

The Law of Attraction enables the manifestation of your thoughts into reality. The Universe will match the vibration of anything you think about with the appropriate occurrences, and subsequently this manifests into your reality.

You are responsible for your own manifestations. Your reality comes directly from your thoughts. Thoughts are things, real things, and not abstract machinations of the mind.

How do you improve your life? Simply by removing all negative thoughts and statements from your mind. Trade the negative comment "I'll never be able to afford a new car" for the positive comment "I will buy a new car."

This sounds difficult, but it is not. By training yourself to catch negative thoughts before you utter them, you create the opportunity to replace that thought with a positive one. It takes less than a week to establish this pattern of thinking. Every time you do this, you are recreating your reality in a positive manner and manifesting what you want out of life.

Another essential practice for improving your reality is letting go of your past. You live in your past, every day of your life. You constantly repeat past behaviors and mistakes, because that is all you know. You let others influence the way you live instead of living the way you want. You've always thought that way, or you've always done things that way. It is learned behavior, and it is limiting behavior.

The key is to cut ties with your past and live in the ever present moment, the NOW. In the now, everything is new. You are not limited by how you did things in the past.

The easiest way to accomplish this is to start with those pesky movies that play over and over in your mind. Generally these instances recall some type of negative emotion on your part, be it blame, shame, anger, guilt, annoyance, and so on. The next time one of these runs through your mind, stop the movie as soon as you realize what it is. Send forgiveness and Love to all the people involved, no matter what they did, and be sure to include yourself in this. It is very important to send yourself Love and forgiveness; this is the most important part of all. Then thank everyone for the lesson they helped you learn, including yourself, and say "I have learned my lesson thanks to all of you and I no longer need to see this ever again." That particular incident will never come back to haunt you.

As you do this time and again, you will feel lighter, and happier. You will find old habits changing and a freedom to approach, to think about things differently. You are manifesting major improvements in your life.

As you manifest more of the things that make you happy into your life, don't get hung up on the "hows" of everything. It is your job to decide what makes you happy. It is the Universe's job to figure out how to deliver it to you. Once you decide what it is you want, take the appropriate steps towards making it a reality.

For instance, suppose you want to take a trip around the world, but you don't have the money. Begin by making positive statements, like "I can't wait to take my trip around the world," and "I'm going to book my trip around the world very soon." Follow these words by investigating which countries you want to visit and begin the planning of your trip. In the meantime, the Universe is investigating all the different ways it can make this come true for you. You may only be able to think of three or four ways to make this possible, but the Universe has an infinite number of ways to deliver this to you. You will find that one day the Universe will hand deliver the missing piece of the puzzle to you, and you will be all set to take your trip.

Here's a great example of manifestation, short and sweet. I had been trying to sell one of my guitar amplifiers, a Mesa Boogie, on Craigslist for almost a year to no avail. The price was right, but no one was biting. I wasn't even getting the usual ridiculous lowball offers! Then one night I was surfing the web, and I came across the Soldano brand of guitar amplifiers, and began thinking about how amazing it would be to have one of them to add to my collection. I fell asleep thinking about it. When I awoke the next morning, I had an email from a guy who wanted to trade me his Soldano amp for my Mesa Boogie amp. We met 4 hours later and completed the trade. Thank you Universe!

This may seem like a minor example of manifestation, and it is. The point is that once you are in the flow of the

Universe, in the ever present NOW, putting out thoughts with vibrations of Love and joy, these types of manifestations become constant. It gets to the point where you find all you have to do is just think about something, and it happens! Life becomes pure magic at this stage. You find you must be careful of what you think. You learn that life is based on your thoughts. Your thoughts become your actions, and your actions result in manifestations.

You live in a truly magical Universe!

CHAPTER TEN-TIME

Time does not exist outside of our third dimension. There is only the eternal NOW, the ever present moment. Past, present and future events all happened at once, and were over in a flash. You lived all of your lives, including the probable ones, and the one you are living right now, simultaneously.

This is a difficult concept to grasp while you are in physical form. Time rules your world. Everyone carries a timepiece of some sort everywhere they go.

Time exists only in our dimension, the third dimension. The critical factor for the installation of time in our dimension is the concept of karma. There can be no cause and effect without time. The effect must always follow the cause, after a delay, so that there is an understandable reason for the effect.

Your ego understands this, and depends on time for its stability. The ego needs time to make sense out of actions. When seemingly random actions are put into the perspective of time, the ego then understands the underlying interactions by placing those actions in the proper sequence using other prior and subsequent actions.

Time controls our lives in another way too. We all live in our pasts while on Earth. Each of us makes decisions based upon our past decisions. Each of us behaves according to our past behaviors. The past is all we know. We react to an event in a certain way because that is the way we have always reacted to that event. We continually relive our past.

Our past determines our future. If you made only good choices in your past, then you will make only good choices going forward. But what if your past decisions and behaviors were not good for you? How do you change that?

Letting go of your past so you are living in the ever present moment is challenging, but very doable once you know the secret. The key to accomplishing this is Love and forgiveness.

We all experience movies in our minds of past experiences that evoke unpleasant emotions, like anger, blame, shame, guilt, and more. These flashbacks occur frequently, because when we think of them, we are always trying to figure out what we could have said or done differently to achieve a different result. There is no need for this. The next time one of these movies pops into your mind, say out loud to everyone involved "I Love you all and I forgive you all. I especially forgive and send Love to myself. Thank you everyone for the lessons I learned from you. I don't need to see this anymore, so goodbye." You may also address each person individually. That movie is now gone from your mind, and will not repeat itself. This is how you stop living in the past and release yourself from the confines of your past actions and decisions.

It can take years to accomplish this, but it is worth every ounce of effort. It will take weeks, maybe months, before this becomes second nature to you. You will reach a point where your mind will intercept these movies before they even begin to play. Once these movies are removed from your thinking, you are free to approach situations differently, from a place of Love and forgiveness. You will find yourself automatically censoring your old way of thinking to allow for new thoughts. Then your habits change. Your life changes. Life becomes easier and more fun. It is a gradual transition. Allow it to happen.

Outside of our third dimensional universe there is no time. Everything- past, present and future- happened simultaneously. Psychics are able to read future events for you because they have already happened. Of course, you may change your future by exercising your free will. For the most part, the future that has happened is the most probable future for you.

When you exercise your free will, you change the timeline you are following. You create new realities. Think of every decision in your life as a choice between going right or left. When you exercise your free will and decide to go right, you continue traveling on your timeline for the duration of this physical existence. But, by not taking the left fork, you also create a new timeline for the left direction. Imagine another "you" taking the left fork and living out that timeline- you have created a probable reality, a parallel timeline. And that "you" also makes decisions about right and left, creating even more timelines. Thus, by the time you die, you have created millions of parallel timelines, ensuring that you lived out every single possible scenario for this incarnation. This assists your learning process. During your Life Review, which takes place after you die, you are able to see the "what ifs?", the roads not taken, because a probable "you" did indeed take those roads. You can see and experience what it would have been like had you decided not to join the military, or not gone to college, or not gotten married. You are able to learn from every possible experience in each physical incarnation.

In this way every probability in your life is fully played out and experienced. You gain valuable knowledge from this.

And what you learn, Source also learns.

CHAPTER ELEVEN- ILLNESS

There is NO illness outside of the Earth. You are perfect outside of your physical lifetimes. The other beings in our Universe know how to manipulate their DNA to cure all illnesses.

Illness occurs through one of three ways. You agree to an illness prior to being born, your mind manifests the illness during the course of your incarnation, or another being enters your body. Remember, there is NO illness outside of the Earth. You are perfect outside of your physical lifetimes.

Some souls agree to contract a specific illness in a particular lifetime to facilitate a learning lesson for another soul. Some illnesses last a short time and some stretch for years, even a lifetime; some are cured and some are not. The more serious illnesses result in death at some point. When making plans for your next physical life, you often decide to experience the loss of a loved one during that lifetime. This makes perfect sense to you as an energy being because you know the "deceased" loved one will be waiting for you when you return home at the end of your physical incarnation.

But, thanks to the veil of amnesia, you don't remember this loss is only temporary, and that is why it is an extremely powerful learning tool. Therefore you experience all the emotions and stages of grief associated with losing a loved one on Earth. In one lifetime you may lose your child during infancy; in another you may lose your child during the teenage years. Your loss may occur from disease or an accident of some kind. By the time your incarnations on Earth are complete, you will have experienced every possible loss imaginable in order to maximize the depth of your lessons and your understanding of Love.

As some of you already know, these are incredibly powerful emotions that stay with you for years, even an entire lifetime. You may feel some kind of responsibility for what happened to your loved one; however you are no more responsible for their death than you are for the sun rising each day. But you cannot realize that due to the veil of amnesia.

Illnesses not agreed to before birth are manifested in your mind during your physical incarnation. The primary reasons for this are negative thoughts and conditioning.

Every cell in your body has a consciousness and intelligence. They are constantly in a state of creation because they live and die. Your cells are replaced constantly. Left to their own devices, your cells are perfect and will always be perfect and you will live a long, healthy life.

But few people are able to live their lives without conflict and negativity. Negative thoughts create situations in the body like stress, which then inhibits the perfect lives of your cells. As a result you get sick. The severity of sickness depends on the degree of negativity involved.

Worry is a key factor in developing serious illness. Worry is essentially a negative thought. When you worry you are thinking the same thought over and over. As you repeat that thought you increase the power of that thought. The vibrations of that thought multiply. The Universe matches it with the appropriate occurrence. Bingo! You have just manifested the very illness you were worried about.

These illnesses can generally be reversed by reversing the thinking process of the individual and the people surrounding the individual. Positive thoughts from everyone help start the healing process. The sick person must allow the healing to take place, not force it. Nothing works in this Universe if you try to force it. "Allow" is one of the most important words in the Universe.

Conditioning plays a huge role in illness. You are told throughout your life that if you go outside during winter without a hat, you will catch a cold. So what happens when you go outside in the snow without a hat? You catch a cold!

We as a society have many, many similar beliefs and they all cause illness merely because we believe them. Don't do (fill in the blank) because it will cause (fill in the blank). Remember, thoughts ARE things. Thoughts are real. Your thoughts have vibrations which go out into the Universe, and the Universe MUST match those vibrations with an appropriate reality.

For instance, if you believe that artificial foodstuffs cause cancer, and you use them on a daily basis, you will most likely develop cancer. You can change your thoughts at any time. You are in control of your thoughts, and your health.

Modern medicine is unable to take care of all our problems. This is where healers come into the picture. Healers have been around for tens of thousands of years, and take a much broader view of a patient's health. Healers include the spiritual body in their assessment of an illness. They know that illness originates in the spirit body, and when it hits critical mass it then manifests in the physical body. A complete physical recovery is not possible without a complete spiritual recovery.

For instance, doctors treat long term pain resulting from a ten year old operation with medicine hoping to make the symptoms disappear, but this does not treat the cause. Most likely they don't know the cause. A healer would know that there is still damage in the spirit body of the patient, and take care of that first. When the spirit body is healed, the physical pain disappears.

The third way illness manifests in a person is through invasion by another being. While healers recognize this as a common occurrence, modern medicine does not.

People develop holes in their spirit bodies through addictions, emotional problems, and abuse. Deceased people who have not crossed over and are still on this plane of existence can spot these holes, and they enter the person's physical body through these holes.

These invasive beings are generally looking for a person to continue their past way of life. A dead addict will search out another addict to continue feeling the rush of the drugs or alcohol. A dead violent person will seek out an abused person and take up residence inside of that person in order to continue its violent actions and thoughts.

When these things happen, physical changes occur in the victim. The beings feed on the energy of the victim, resulting in sickness of varying degrees. Mental changes occur too, because now there are two consciousnesses occupying the same mind.

The healer knows that in these cases he must call in someone specialized in depossession work, such as a shaman. The shaman knows that these invasive beings thrive on negative energy, so he must approach them from a place of pure Love. There is a certain procedure that is followed to remove the beings and help them cross over into the Light. The procedure is non-confrontational and generally very successful. The victim feels better immediately after the procedure is completed and continues to improve until he/she is back to normal.

CHAPTER TWELVE-
ACCIDENTS AND COINCIDENCES

There is no such thing as a coincidence. Events do not occur by happenstance. Everything happens perfectly, for a reason. Coincidences are the Universe's way of responding to your thoughts.

A coincidence is the Universe providing the answer to "how" something will happen. You only know a few ways to make things happen; the Universe has an infinite number of ways to manifest events. That chance meeting you had with just the right individual who can help you with your business, that seemingly came out of the clear blue sky, was the Universe answering your thoughts for assistance. Thoughts are things, and the Universe always answers your call.

Accidents do not occur by happenstance either. Accidents are learning experiences for you.

Perhaps someone was injured due to your negligence. Maybe you turned away for just a second, and something terrible happened. You then spend days, weeks, months, even years beating yourself up over it. You blame yourself for everything that occurred. It may have changed your life, or someone else's life.

While you do learn important lessons from these situations, the greatest lesson you can learn is forgiveness. Forgive yourself for the blame you feel. Forgive yourself for the shame and guilt you feel. Realize and understand that the person who was injured as a result of the accident agreed to this before you both were born. You both agreed to it. Many people do not understand this and spend their entire lives in misery, carrying a huge weight of guilt, blame and shame for one occurrence years, even decades earlier. Send all involved Love and forgiveness, especially yourself, and go on with your life.

This is much easier said than done, but it is important to know even as you are going through the stages of grief. Feel the emotions, embrace them, and when the grieving is complete, bring out the Love and forgiveness for all, including yourself.

CHAPTER THIRTEEN- DEATH

Our society has it backwards.

We celebrate birth, and mourn death. Because of the veil of amnesia, we don't understand that death is a homecoming, a time of celebration. We have completed out work on Earth, and it's time to go home.

Birth should be a time of mourning. You have left home to experience physical reality on Earth, and the veil of amnesia ensures you won't remember what you left behind. A home where you are perpetually young and perfect. A home where every thought manifests instantly. A home where negativity doesn't exist. A world filled with Love.

And now it's bad pun time. We are all "scared to death" of dying.

What are we scared of? What causes such an incredibly powerful reaction when the topic of death comes up in conversation? As a society we would rather sweep it under the rug than talk about it.

We think death is final. The end. We think we are humans with a spiritual side. We don't know that we are actually souls with a temporary human side. We don't understand what happens when that final moment comes.

We find it hard to believe the people who have near-death experiences. Since no one has ever risen from the dead to explain what happens, these people are the next best thing.

They have been declared medically dead, yet they have come back to us. Some say they were told "It's not your time yet." Some say they were given a choice, and made a conscious decision to return to Earth for many reasons. The fantastic descriptions of the tunnel of Light, the overwhelming sensations of peace and Love, our loved ones waiting for us- we just don't buy it.

Why do we have such a tough time with death? The main reason is that we, as a society, have forgotten the rituals of the life cycle that humanity used for tens of thousands of years. The ancient rituals marking birth, adolescence, and death were the backbone of tribal life. Our ancestors, thanks to the tribal shamans, understood the basic connection between man and Source, knowledge that has disappeared from our modern societies. These ancient rituals ensured that information about Source remained integrated within the community for all to understand.

The tribal shaman, who spent much of his time in non-ordinary reality, reaching out to the spirits for guidance, understood death. He knew death was the sign that an individual's work on this plane was completed. He knew death meant that person was going home. The shaman shared that knowledge with the members of the tribe. Elders held special status in these times, and were celebrated for their knowledge and experience. When a tribal member was on his deathbed, he was secure in his knowledge of what was about to happen and where he was going.

We have lost that knowledge. Modern society has replaced the shaman with doctors and weather satellites. We have lost touch with nature, nature that we used to live in for hundreds of thousands of years. Instead of walking barefoot on the ground and sleeping under the stars, we now live in massive brick structures in cities where little if any grass is to be seen anywhere.

Death is nothing more than a seamless transition from the third dimension to your home dimension. There is no loss of consciousness when your earthly body ceases to function; you do not fade to black forever. Your consciousness, which is composed of eternal energy, merely leaves the human shell and proceeds home through the tunnel of Light. All physical problems are gone, and you return to a state of perpetual youth. There is no illness. There is no need for air or food. Your thoughts manifest instantly. You communicate with everyone telepathically. You remain in this state of perfection until you choose to reincarnate again.

In the event of death caused by something other than old age, your soul will generally leave your body prior to actual physical death. For instance, if death is due to an automobile accident, your soul will depart your body a split second before impact.

If your body is in an irreversible coma, you may leave your body hours, or even days before your body dies. I experienced this first hand when my father-in-law passed away from complications resulting from outliving a liver transplant. He was in a coma and I felt him transition a full 24 hours before his physical body died. When I walked into the funeral home for his wake, I immediately heard my father-in-law joyously yelling in my ears "You were right!! You were right!! I feel great!!" I was able to pass that along to the relatives, helping them feel better.

The deceased communicate with us in many ways to let us know they are fine and not to worry about them. They do this in small ways, like a wisp of a familiar fragrance wafting by, or hearing their favorite song on the radio as you are thinking of them. Be on the lookout for these signs, and you will be surprised how often you notice them.

CHAPTER FOURTEEN-
PSYCHIC ABILITIES

You have the ability to perform the entire spectrum of psychic abilities. After all, what is considered "psychic" on Earth is your normal way of life when home. Telepathy, telekinesis, healing, levitation, astral projection, remote viewing, instant manifestation, these abilities and more are normal when you are home.

On Earth, you are born with the veil of amnesia, so you cannot remember you have these abilities. Some people are born with certain psychic abilities in order to help others on Earth. Some people are born with full sight, and can see and talk to dead people. Some people can tell future events, although such readings are based on the client's probable timeline at the time of the reading and can seem way off base if the client exercises free will, thus changing his or her future.

Some people are born healers. They are able to remove pain and long term problems that modern medicine is incapable of doing.

Young children often have imaginary playmates that they can see and you cannot. These playmates are deceased children who have come back to play. The reason a child can see them is the child has not yet been fully brainwashed by society/parents/teachers that these things are impossible and cannot happen. They will continue to see the spirits until convinced otherwise.

There are introductory psychic classes in most every town that teach you how to "be" psychic. For most people it is a matter of turning off the chatterbox in their heads, meditating, and allowing the information to flow. It takes time and practice.

When I started out, I attended a mediumship development circle headed by a wonderful woman named Gerri. She was very supportive to all of us. But while others were channeling dead people, I was channeling dead animals! I would come up with 3 or 4 deceased animals each class who were pets of my fellow students. This was one of the early indications that shamanism was my calling.

Look online for metaphysical classes near you and attend a few. You will be amazed by what you learn from these classes. The best part of the classes is that it brings you in touch with like minded people, and some of them may turn into lifelong friends. It's a terrific experience!

REFERENCES

The following books are a representation of the many wonderful resources available to further your understanding of the concepts presented in this book. I hope these books lead you to other books and conversations about the topics that interest you.

Aguirre, Cliff. (1984). The Death Transition. San Bernadino, CA: Williams and Gold Communication. A description of the death process.

Archangel Ariel, channeled by Tashira Tachi-ren. (1990). What Is Lightbody? Lithia Springs, GA: World Tree Press. A manual for Lightworkers.

Foundation for Inner Peace. (2007). A Course In Miracles. Mill Valley, CA: Foundation for Inner Peace. A complete method for letting go of your past.

Hicks, Esther & Jerry. (2006). The Law of Attraction: The basics of the teachings of Abraham. Carlsbad, CA: Hay House , Inc. A full description of the Law of Attraction. Esther Hicks channels a collective consciousness named Abraham, who explains the Law of Attraction.

Hicks, Esther & Jerry. (2008). Money, and the Law of Attraction: Learning to attract wealth, health and happiness. Carlsbad, CA: Hay House, Inc. More channeled information from Abraham.

Hicks, Esther & Jerry. (2007). The Astonishing Power of Emotions: Let your feelings be your guide. Carlsbad, CA: Hay House, Inc. More channeled information from Abraham.

Hicks, Esther & Jerry. (2009). The Vortex: Where the Law of Attraction assembles all cooperative relationships. Carlsbad, CA: Hay House, Inc. More channeled information from Abraham.

Moore, Tom T. (2006). The Gentle Way: A self-help guide for those who believe in angels. Flagstaff, AZ: Light Technology Publishing. A precise way to ask for help from your angels, with a complete description.

Newton, Michael. (1995). Journey of Souls. Woodbury, MN: Llewellyn Publications. In depth descriptions of our life between Earthly lives.

Newton, Michael. (2008). Destiny of Souls. Woodbury, MN: Llewellyn Publications. More information about our life between Earthly lives.

Renard, Gary R. (2004). The Disappearance of the Universe: Straight talk about illusions, past lives, religion, sex, politics, and the miracles of forgiveness. Carlsbad, CA: Hay House Publishing, Inc. The spiritual awakening of the author with help from his guides.

Roberts, Jane. (1970). The Seth Material: The spiritual teacher that launched the new age. Manhasset, NY: New Awareness Network, Inc. Useful information about our Earthly lives from a consciousness named Seth as channeled by Jane Roberts in the 1960s.

Roberts, Jane. (1972). Seth Speaks: The eternal validity of the soul. San Rafael, CA: Amber-Allen Publishing. More useful information from Seth.

Roberts, Jane. (1977). The "Unknown" Reality, Volume One. San Rafael, CA: Amber-Allen Publishing. More useful information from Seth.

Roberts, Jane. (1974). The Nature of Personal Reality: Specific, practical techniques for solving everyday problems and enriching the life you know. San Rafael, CA: Amber-Allen Publishing. More useful information from Seth.

Spangler, David. (2010). Subtle Worlds: An explorer's field notes. Everett, WA: Lorian Press. Establishing contact with non-physical life forms.

Stubbs, Tony. (1991). An Ascension Handbook. Livermore, CA: Oughten House Publications. Contains many useful exercises for helping with your ascension to Source.

Toy, Atala Dorothy. (2009), We Are Not Alone: A complete guide to interdimensional cooperation. San Francisco, CA: Weiser Books. A detailed explanation of energy and multidimensional communications.

Wolf, Fred Alan. (2004). The Yoga of Time Travel: How the mind can defeat time. Wheaton, IL: Quest Books. A physicist's explanation of time and how it works.

ABOUT THE AUTHOR

Brad "Little Frog" Hudson is a well known shamanic practitioner, multidimensional energy healer, teacher, bestselling author, and southern-style barbecue fanatic . He received his medicine name, "Little Frog", from Spirit during his first vision quest, a four day/night solo fast in Vermont's Green Mountain wilderness.

His shamanic and healing website is www.littlefroghealing.com. Little Frog works with people and animals, both locally and long distance.

Little Frog resides in Westford, Massachusetts, with his wife Karen, son Robbie, and their two dogs, Tessie and Rondo.

OTHER BOOKS BY BRAD "LITTLE FROG" HUDSON:

Shamanic Depossession and Other True Healing Miracles

Vision Quests: True Stories From the Wilderness

www.ingramcontent.com/pod-product-compliance
Lightning Source LLC
Chambersburg PA
CBHW031332040426
42443CB00005B/314

9780990836827